An Exquisite Inconvenience

Emma Griffiths

BookLeaf Publishing

India | USA | UK

Presentation by *BookLeaf Publishing*

Web: www.bookleafpub.com

E-mail: info@bookleafpub.com

ISBN: 9789357616751

First edition 2023

In honour of Archie Cole who is my sunshine.

PREFACE

This book was born, much like my son, in the early morning after a restless night.

Only You

I did not know I needed you
I did not know a love so pure would consume
me
I did not know the nights are long but weeks are
truly short
I did not know a joy like this was true
I did not know that I could be so powerful
I did not know my soul would ache for you
when we were apart
I did not know that I could be the calm amongst
the storm
Only you could teach me this

Only I

My midnight eyes are heavy but so full is my heart
I can tell already that I don't ever want to part
Motherhood can be confusing; we really need to slumber
But please wake up I miss you my darling little wonder
Lying snuggling in my arms, your gaze is fixed on mine
My body gives you nourishment and I revel in the calm
When life is overwhelming and not what you've known
Just remember I'll always be your home
It's only I at night, with you and our special time
To cuddle and reflect, and let our true bond shine
A bond like no other right at Mama's breast
It's only I in this moment who can comfort you the best

I'm The Winner

My new baby, you inspire me to write.
How I love the way you smile and radiate your
light
How do I love you? It's impossible to count the
ways
I see time flashing past as you grow in every
way
I love your twinkling bright blue eyes
You're my jackpot and my biggest prize
You invade my mind throughout the day and
night
I wouldn't want it any other way- that's right!
You've given me life and given me purpose
All that's left is hitting high targets
Your Great Grandparents are heavenly angels
My loss of them was so so painful
But they've sent me the best
They picked you for me and that is blessed
Every day we spend together
Becomes a memory to treasure
A place in Mama's heart is always kept for you

Us Vs Them

My sweet baby boy how little you are
You need cuddles and kisses and time galore
They tell me to train you and schedule you out
But my heart tells me to just block them all out
I instinctively know what you need right now
Even if that means I'm met with a raised brow
They're quick to judge and freely instruct
But this Mama needs space to grow so they can
get fucked
They laugh at me for my hopes and ideas
And pounce on them like a clan of hyenas
Sorting through advice is slow progress
I don't want to rush an inevitable process
They tell me I'm too this or too that, or not the
right way
But you are not in their arms at the end of the
day
You're only little for a very short time
But remember I'll be your Mama for a lifetime

Changed For The Better

I was a woman before but now a Mother
A very slow burn turned me into the other
My body and mind needed time to recover
The fourth trimester was our little buffer
This transformation did change me to be tougher
And your sole existence makes my heart flutter
Everyday we learn about our world and each
other
Feeling how deep this love goes makes me
shudder
I daydream lots and wonder what will be your
favorite colour
And one day I hope to hear you proudly say
that's my Mama
Be patient as I'm still a work in progress
But I'll be the best Mum for you, not less!

The Village

I envisioned a particular village to hold you tight
This is not what I had planned but it will do just
right
Your bonus big brother that you'll share at home
And not feel like you are ever alone
You lost dear old ones before you were born
But now they're in heaven above to adore
You have Grandma and Grandad times two by
the sea
And Great Aunts and Uncles who are
surrounded by trees
You have cousins from a distance
And friends turned family close with insistence
You have your Mama and your Daddy
And hopefully soon a pet to call kitty
You'll make friends along the way
To keep us company and pave the way
Some will come and some will go
Some people are a blessing and others a lesson
Hold tight to the ones who standby in thick or
thin
Because if friends are the currency you can win!

New Mum, New Fun

Before I was your Mum
I slept all night and then had some fun
But I had never loved beyond a measure
Or known a smile to be the greatest pleasure
Or held someone for hours because I couldn't
stand to be apart
I never had my arms full and a bursting heart
I never knew someone so small could make such
a big difference
I never knew this new love would be so
significant
I'm a new Mum
And having you is like a home run

A New Dynamic

Blending families is not for the faint hearted
Your path will indeed be bombarded
You're a chess piece
Dancing around to keep the peace
The game board is scattered with rules that are
not your own
You may be surrounded but feel all alone
Some of the days are Herculean
Even though a family is to be won
Cooking up a storm of people
Pop goes the weasel
Put a kind and honest woman into the mix
Add one and another and it's a stew of pickup
sticks
Slowly stir in patience
Add a knock of flirtatious
Many rivers are merging
And hearts and minds surging
Trying to come together in a circle
A form that never ends
It may look worn and broken
But underneath are the ingredients to a love
potion

By My Side

You are by my side all day and all night
But I don't want it any other way
The overwhelming surge of love
Hits me like a tsunami wave
I could do you alone, if alone I'd be
You consume my thoughts and actions
It mostly came to me as raw instinct
And some I had to learn
Before you, I used to judge and think this was all so cliché
But until you've walked this path
You'll never understand that being apart is like forgetting to breathe
If you do, you just can't do it for long

Growth

Sun and moon shining
Blooming rage and peace at once
A transformation

New Path

Imperfect but right
The leaf waiting to be turned
Twisting path ahead

What Is Love?

It's late nights and early mornings
You're sent by the angels from above
It's coping with all the risks and warnings
It's being the arms of a protector
Having the remote just out of reach
Soothing the cries; the job of a director
Even the tiredness sees you sweet as a peach
Love is in your eyes, your smile and down to
your cute chubby toes
It's being organized with a fresh outfit
It's being the woman that was and will be all
superimposed
It's not letting others doubt it
Love drives
And love survives

The Show

13

Welcoming fireworks
From earth putting on a show
Mediocrity

Through My Eyes

You never understand life until it grows inside
you
Then when the timer goes off
Your heart and soul are on the outside of you
I used to be the one to scoff
But until you walk in these shoes
It simply doesn't make sense
You are the shield to the blues
Being enthralled by you is common sense

Ain't No Other

15

I'm given patience and grace and understood
Strangers kind like friends from childhood
It's simple, there ain't no other hood like
motherhood!

Why?

Why like this, is it by your design?
Can't you tell it's not ever benign?
There needs to be less and also more
Not enough time has passed to be a chore
Why can't the story come from cloud nine?

Breathe

Come to the seaside
Rest among the shores and breathe
Home away from home

Let It Go

Let it go with grace and maturity
Push through the thought of impurity
The babe in your arms is as sweet as pure honey
Cuddly and distracting like a little bunny
Who knew I could be so lucky
Strap yourself in for the ride in the buggy
Remember the little one is the key
No matter if in the gully or if by the sea

More

We will be so much more
My eyes are open and my feet are ready
I need some mistakes to make me steady
But for now let's ride on and explore

Counting On

One two, let's more than survive
Three four, let us strive to thrive
Five six, kiss on the lips
Seven eight, watch the eclipse
Nine ten, there's endless revives

Exquisite

Change is refreshing
Mother Nature's best secret
Exquisite blessing yes!

www.ingramcontent.com/pod-product-compliance
Lightning Source LLC
LaVergne TN
LVHW050300200726
843509LV00015B/3072